CHINA'S LAST EMPEROR WAS 2 YEARS OLD!

History Books for Kids | Children's Asian History

Speedy Publishing LLC

40 E. Main St. #1156

Newark, DE 19711

www.speedypublishing.com

Copyright 2017

All Rights reserved. No part of this book may be reproduced or used in any way or form or by any means whether electronic or mechanical, this means that you cannot record or photocopy any material ideas or tips that are provided in this book.

The last emperor of China was only a baby the first time he was crowned! Let's find out how that happened, and what happened next, at the end of Imperial China.

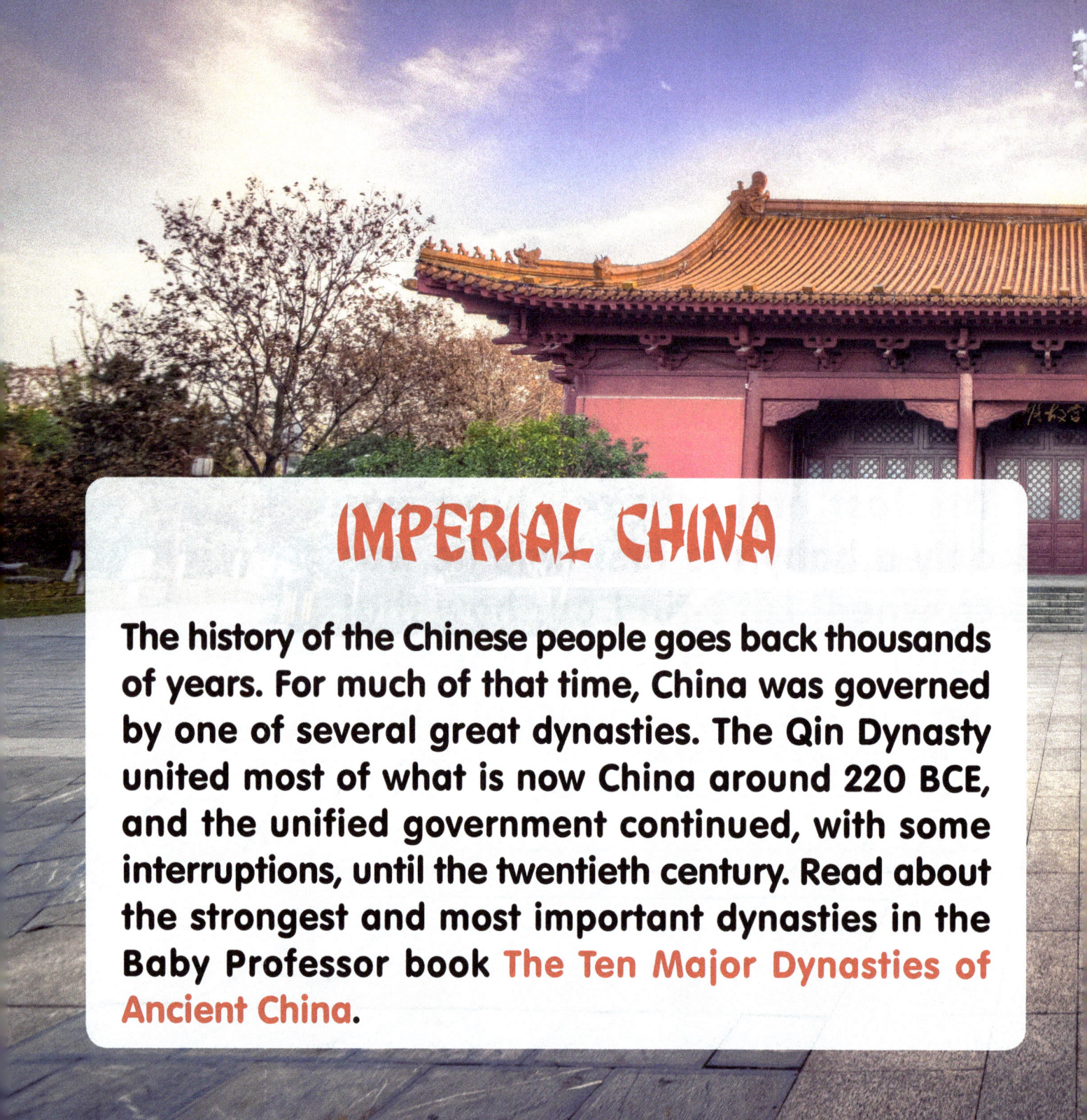

IMPERIAL CHINA

The history of the Chinese people goes back thousands of years. For much of that time, China was governed by one of several great dynasties. The Qin Dynasty united most of what is now China around 220 BCE, and the unified government continued, with some interruptions, until the twentieth century. Read about the strongest and most important dynasties in the Baby Professor book The Ten Major Dynasties of Ancient China.

ANCIENT TOWN IN LIJIANG, YUNNAN

But in the early 1900s there was great pressure for change. Chinese people could see how other countries had moved ahead economically and in other ways under more democratic governments, and they wanted the same for their own country. There were other forces in play, including people who did not mind the idea of an emperor—but wanted to be that emperor themselves!

THE LAST EMPEROR'S SHORT REIGN

When the man who became the last emperor of China was born, in 1906, the emperor on the throne was the Guangxu Emperor of the Manchu Dynasty. The real ruler of China, however, was the Empress Dowager Cixi. She had ruled China, no matter who was emperor, since 1861!

MARBLE BOAT OF EMPRESS DOWAGER CIXI

TOMB OF EMPRESS DOWAGER CIXI

In 1908, the Guangxu Emperor was poisoned and died. The Empress Dowager selected the two-year-old prince to be the next emperor, evidently thinking he would be easy for her to manipulate and that she could go on being in charge for many more years. However, the Empress Dowager died just one day later!

THE ANCIENT ROYAL PALACES OF THE FORBIDDEN CITY

In December, 1908, Aisin-Gioro Puyi, just two years old, was enthroned as the Xuantong Emperor. The Dowager Empress Longyu, hoping to gain control of the nation, formally adopted the infant emperor into her family and isolated him from the family of his birth.

From then until 1912, Puyi lived in the Forbidden City, the huge walled area of palaces and parks in Beijing, the capital.

PUYI IN DRAGON CHAIR

He had no access to power, although he discovered that his servants had to obey any command he gave them...and that he could have them beaten! Only Wen-Chao Wang, the woman who acted as a mother to him, had any power over him.

A general, Yuan Shikai was campaigning for a more modern China as part of what became known as the Xinhai Revolution. Behind the scenes, be bribed the Dowager Empress Longyu with a huge amount of silver and a promise to let her live if she helped depose the Xuantong Emperor. She agreed, and suddenly, in February of 1912, the child emperor's reign was over. He was only six years old, and he was not allowed to leave the Forbidden City.

ANTIQUE CHINA SILVER DOLLAR COINS WITH YUAN SHIKAI FACE

General Yuan declared a Republic of China, with himself as president. He continued that way until 1915, when he declared that he was actually the emperor, the first one of a new dynasty. However, three months later he fell ill and died.

In 1917, a leader named Zhang Xun tried to seize power. He restored Puyi as emperor. But eleven days later another leader, Duan Qirui, vetoed the return of the child emperor.

In 1924, when Puyi was 18, another leader of the Republic of China, Fen Yuxian, forced the former emperor to leave the Forbidden City.

A PUPPET EMPEROR

Japan offered refuge to Puyi and he moved first into the Japanese embassy in Beijing and then to a Japanese-controlled area in the north of China. The Japanese were enemies of the Han Chinese, who largely controlled the Xinhai Revolution, and they promised Puyi that they would put him back on his throne. Their plan was to use him as the public face of the government of China that Japan would control.

In 1931, Japan invaded and conquered Manchuria, the northern area of China from which Puyi's family had come. They made Puyi the emperor of a new country, Manchukuo, which Japan continued to control.

FORMER MANCHUKUO STATE DEPARTMENT, CHINA

PUYI AT MANCHUKUO

Until 1945, Puyi continued as a leader without power, surrounded by Chinese "advisers" who were sympathetic to Japan and were the people who made the real decisions. He even had to sign a document agreeing that if he had a son, the son would be educated in Japan.

CHINESE SOLDIERS MARCHING

Japan and China were at war from 1937, with Japan occupying much of China, including many of its major cities. In 1941 this conflict became part of the much larger World War II. Japan was on the side of Germany and Italy; and China was part of the Allied governments including Great Britain, France, the Soviet Union, and the United States.

SOVIET UNION FLAG

Toward the end of the war the Soviet Union invaded and conquered Manchukuo. As Japan surrendered, ending the war, Puyi was captured by the Soviet army. He was kept as a prisoner of war until 1949.

In China, a communist revolution finally defeated the Republic of China in 1948. The last remnant of the Republic of China continues on the island of Taiwan. The Soviet Union transferred the former emperor of China, now 43 years old, to Chinese control. Learn more about this new movement in the Baby Professor book What is Communism?

LIFE IN THE NEW CHINA

Puyi was sent to a re-education camp. Re-education camps were partly punishment for people who had served Japan, Manchukuo, or the republican government, and partly a way to prepare these people to live in the new reality of Communist China. Puyi spent ten years at the Fushun War Criminals Management Center.

BOTANICAL GARDEN

In 1959, Puyi, now 54 years old, was released from the center. He made public speeches in support of the Communist government of China and denouncing crimes of the imperial past. He returned to Beijing and got work there as a gardener at the botanical gardens.

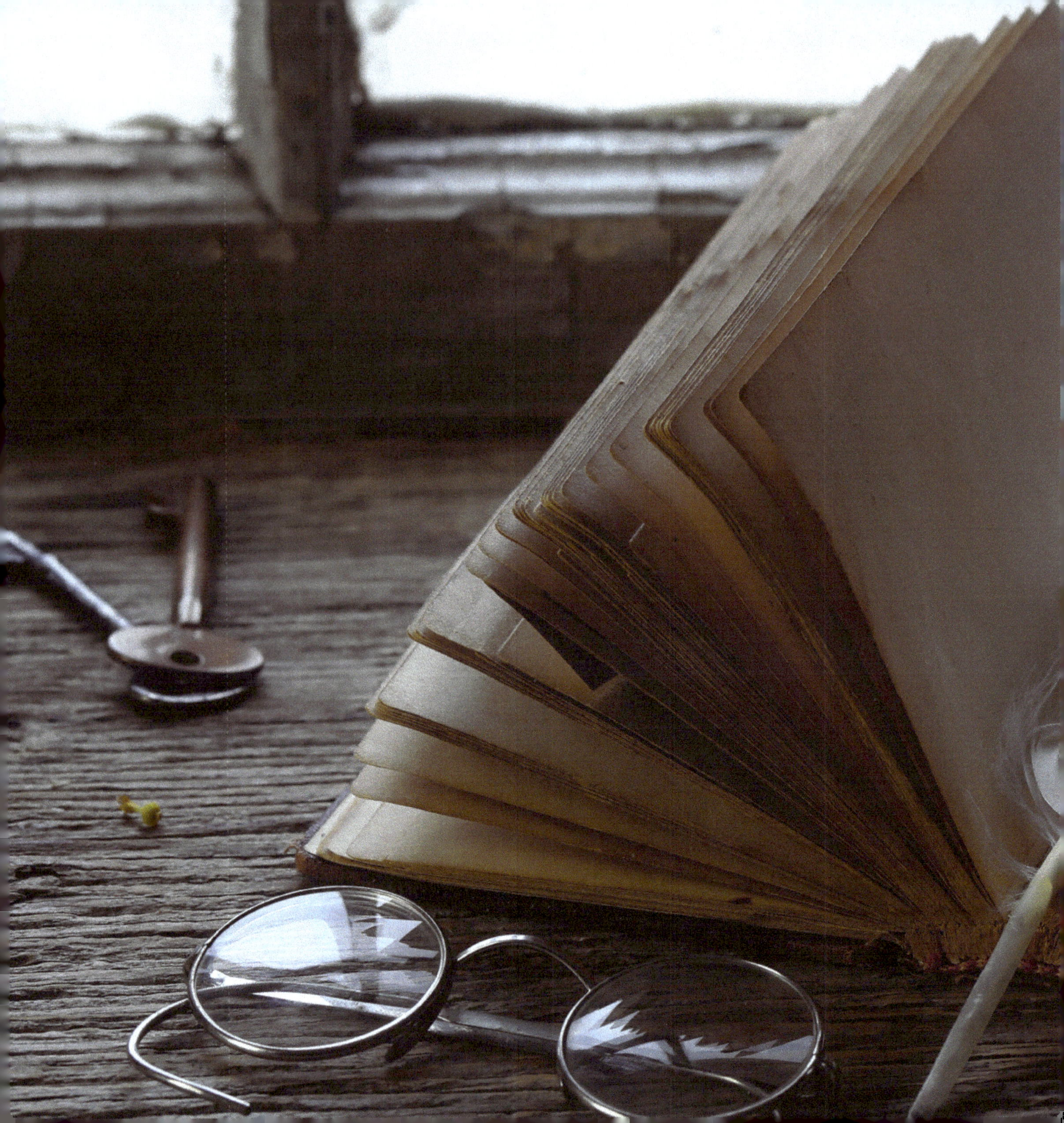

From 1964 Puyi worked as an editor and writer, as well as continuing his gardening work. He published the story of his life, From Emperor to Citizen.

CLOSING YEARS

In 1966 there was a new purification of Chinese society called the Cultural Revolution. Anybody suspected of not being loyal enough to the Communist nation and Communist teaching was jailed or sent to camps for re-education. Puyi became a target for criticism as being a symbol of Imperial China. The government arrested him for his own protection, and he lost his freedom yet again.

MUSEUM OF THE CONGRESS OF THE CHINESE COMMUNIST PARTY

BEIJING, CHINA

At age 61, in 1967, Aisin-Gioro Puyi died of cancer. He had been emperor three times in two countries, but never really had power. He died in Beijing, the city of his birth.

FACTS ABOUT THE LAST EMPEROR

- Puyi was made emperor three times, twice in China and once in Manchukuo. At no time, though, did he have any real power.
- He was the youngest person ever to become emperor of China, at the age of two years and ten months.

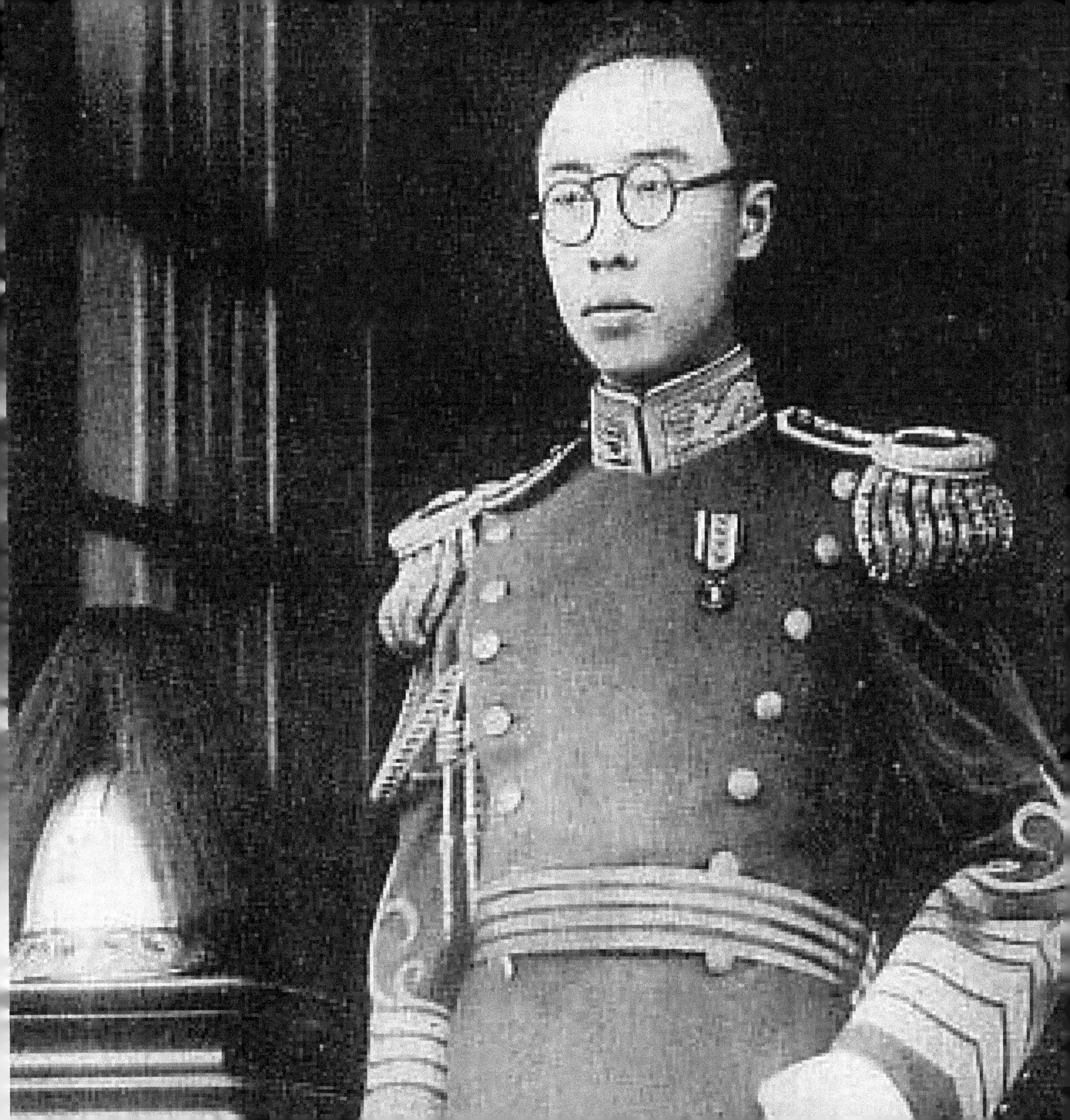

大清國當今聖母皇太后萬歲萬歲萬萬歲

EMPRESS DOWAGER LONGYU

- The end of Puyi's first time as emperor was by an order the Empress Dowager Longyu signed. There was no battle or conquest, and no decision by a court or government.
- Puyi was the first Chinese emperor to learn English. He was also the first to wear Western clothing rather than traditional Chinese robes. He took the name Henry, which his English tutor chose for him.

- Chinese emperors traditionally wore their hair long, tied into a queue that reached down to the middle of their backs. When "Henry" began to wear Western clothing and understand the ways of the modern world, he had his queue cut off and adopted a Western haircut.
- Puyi was married five times. His second wife, Wenxiu, divorced him in 1931, making him the first emperor to be divorced.

CHILDREN WEARING TRADITIONAL CHINESE CLOTHING

MAO ZEDONG

- Mao Zedong, Chairman of the Chinese Communist Party and the most powerful man in Communist China, ordered that Puyi be allowed to live as a normal Chinese citizen after the last emperor emerged from his re-education camp.

- **Puyi was active in national organizations. He was a member of the fourth National Committee of the Chinese People's Political Consultative Conference.**

CHINESE PEOPLE'S POLITICAL CONSULTATIVE CONFERENCE

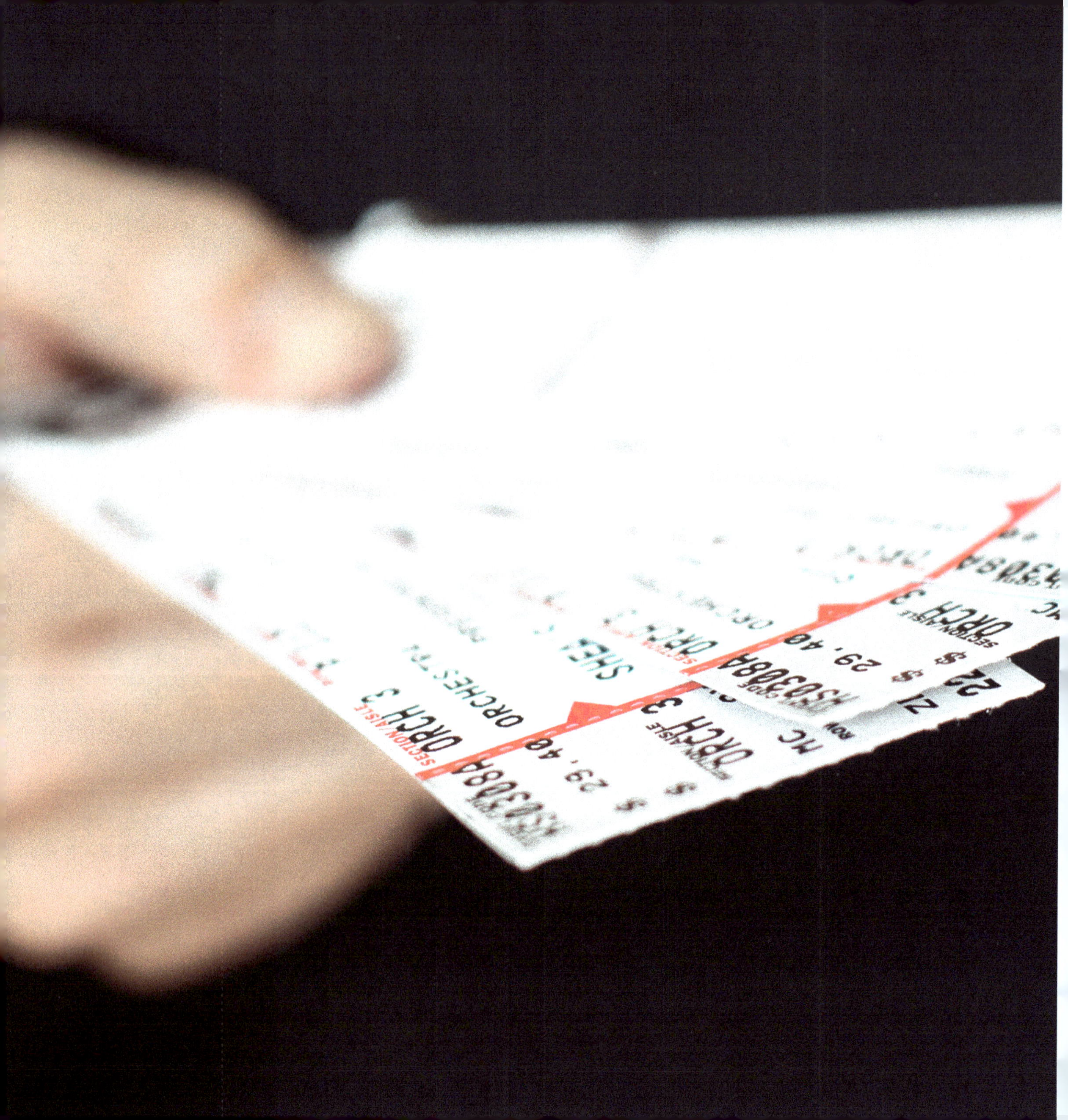
ORCH 3
SECTION/AISLE
ORCHESTRA
$ 29.40
21
22

- **As well as being a gardener at the Beijing Botanical Gardens, Puyi shared the duty of selling tickets to visitors.**

- **Puyi lived through the end of Imperial China, the birth of the Republic of China, the Second Sino-Japanese War, World War II, and the creation of the People's Republic of China. Although he held an impressive title during some of these events, in reality he had little power and was more of an observer than an actor on the stage of history.**

JAPANESE RESIDENTS OF BEIJING, CHINA

BERNARDO BERTOLUCCI

- **A movie, The Last Emperor, introduced Puyi's story to a wide audience in 1987. The epic, directed by Italian Bernardo Bertolucci, won nine Academy Awards in 1988, including Best Picture.**

LEARN ABOUT CHINESE CULTURE AND HISTORY

Aisin-Gioro Puyi had no idea, as he was growing up, how suddenly and sharply everything would change in China. He expected things to go on as they had for thousands of years. Read about the pageant of Chinese history, and why the last emperor would have thought that way, in Baby Professor books like Who Built the Great Wall of China?, Kublai Khan: China's Mongol Emperor, and How did your Chinese Ancestors Live?

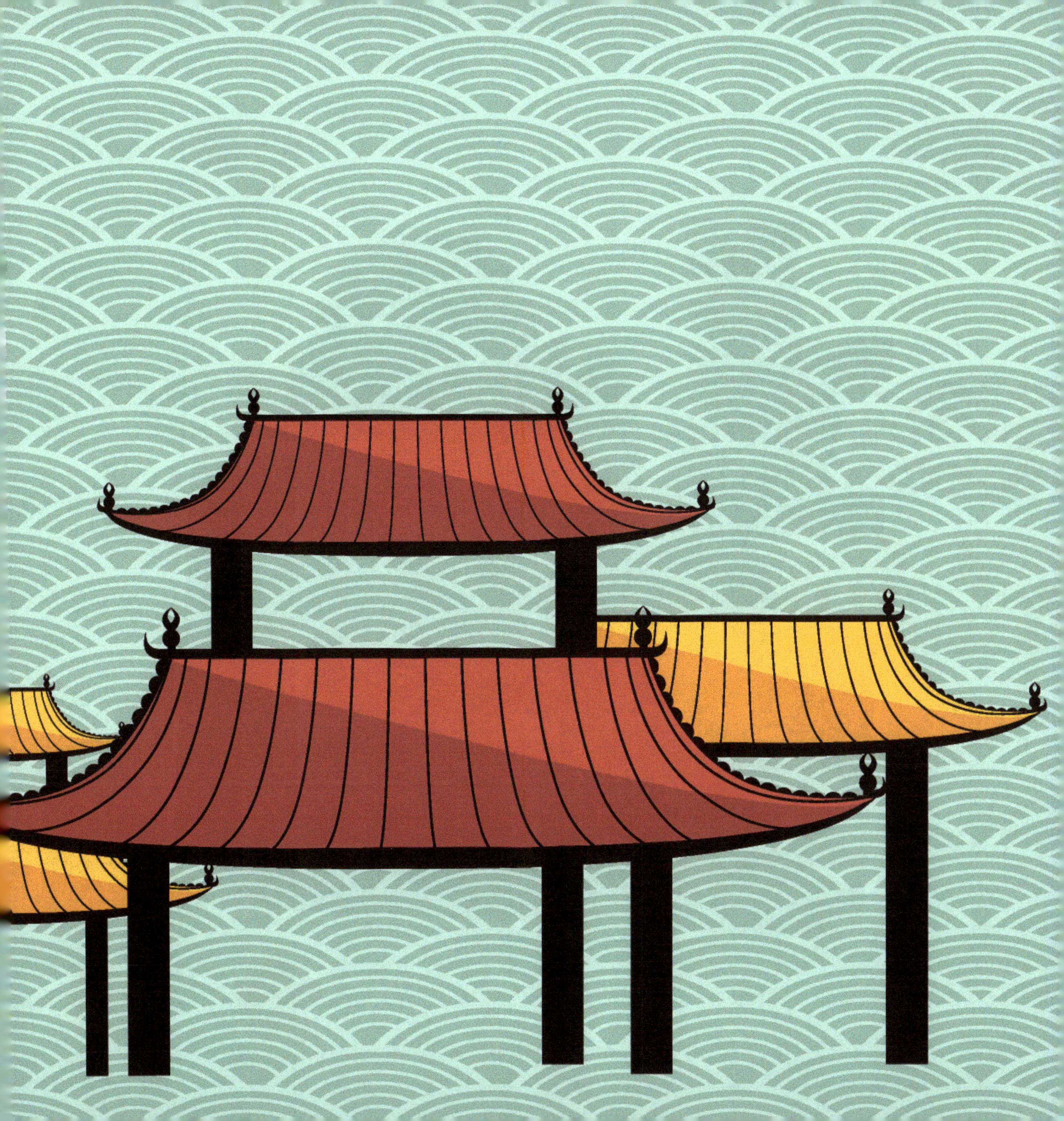

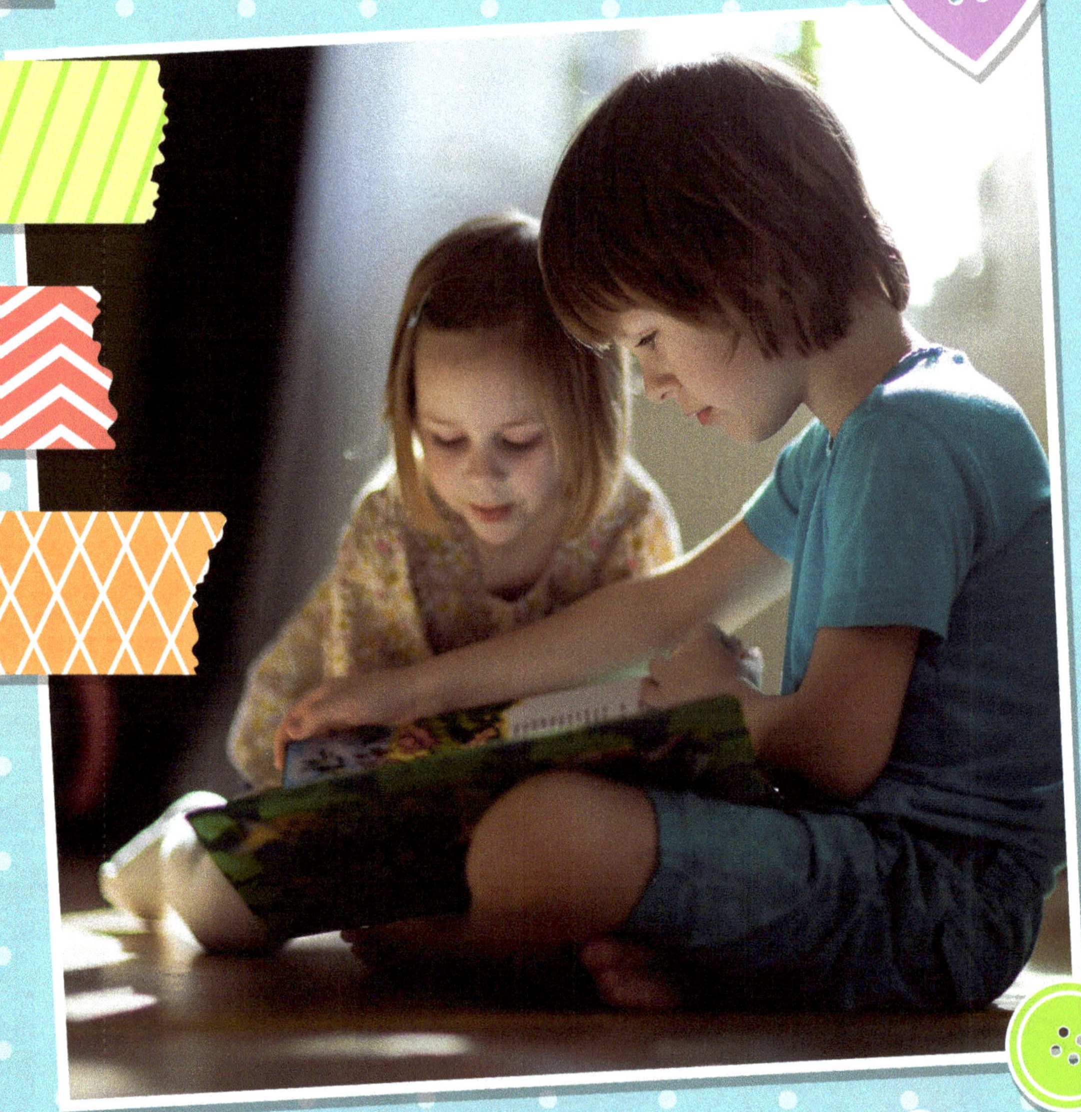

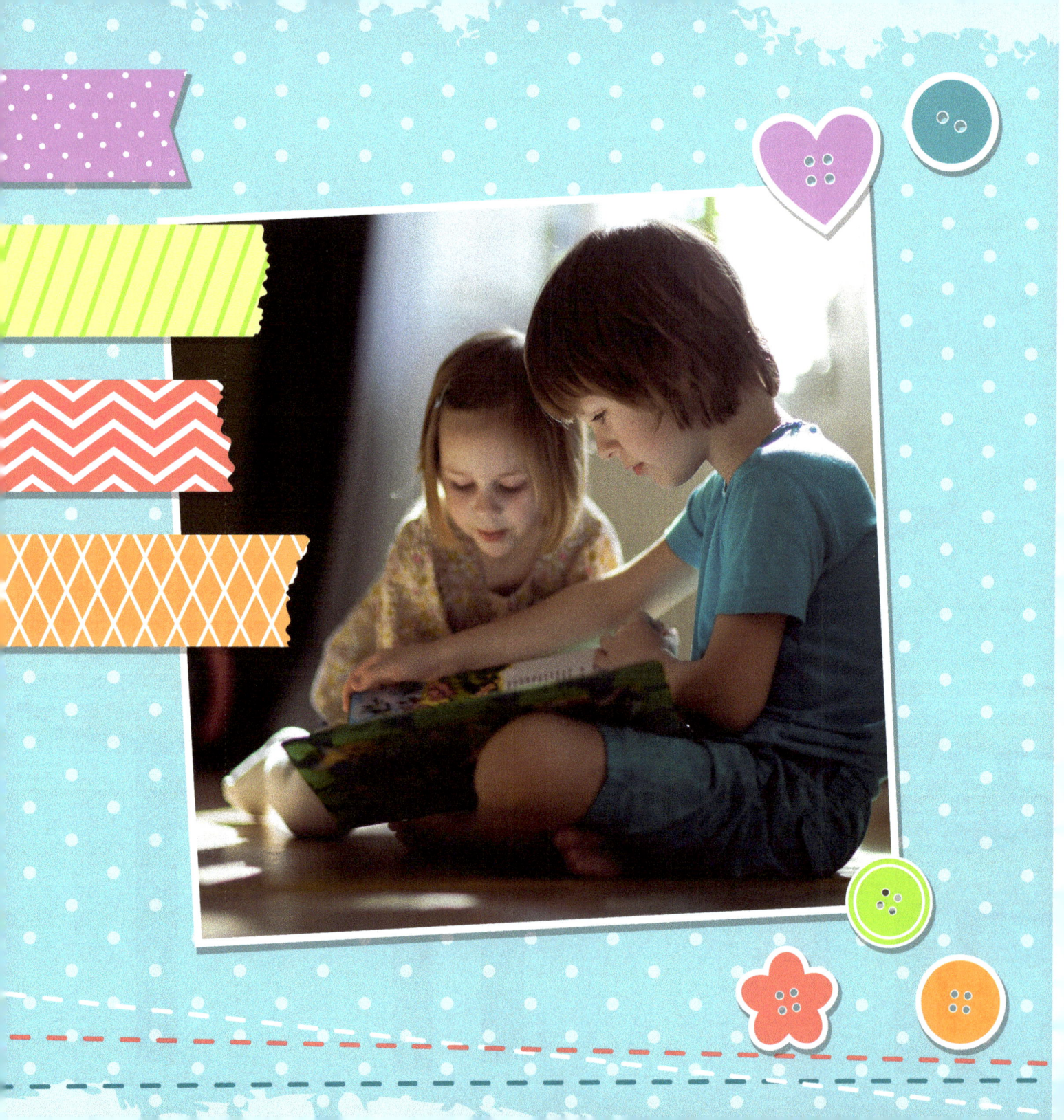

Visit

BABY PROFESSOR
EDUCATION KIDS

www.BabyProfessorBooks.com

to download Free Baby Professor eBooks and view our catalog of new and exciting Children's Books

Milton Keynes UK
Ingram Content Group UK Ltd.
UKHW051124030924
447802UK00003B/54